longer, as was pretended at the commencement of the
question, a revision, a modification of the penal code
in Egypt which is now demanded, but the full and
complete introduction of the Tanzimat. Many persons, who are ignorant of the usually complicated
character of questions relating to affairs in the East,
may ask in what respects the introduction of the *Tanzimat* into Egypt would prove an obstacle to the
establishment of the railway. This inquiry is a very
natural one; but these persons will themselves see
how nearly related these two matters are, how identical
indeed they become, when we shall have given them,
as we intend to do presently, a sketch of the nature of
the Tanzimat, and pointed out all the consequences of
the claims of the Porte; let it suffice for us at this
moment to fix the epoch at which Constantinople put
forward its first demand.

During the first two years of his government, the
Viceroy, maintaining with perfect submission his
friendly relations towards the Porte, occupied himself
with the internal administration of the country. From
the beginning the transit across Egypt had attracted
his attention : in the constant passage of travellers to
and from India he saw a source of wealth, of prosperity for his country, a means of civilization for the
people that he governed : he then applied himself to
the improvement of the transit ; no expense was spared
by him, no outlay appeared to him too great. It is natural

that in this state of mind the idea of constructing a railway should present itself to him. He communicated his views to certain persons who possessed his confidence, and among others to his late minister, Artin Bey, on whom he thought he could rely, but who, according to his custom, did not fail at the very instant to apprise the Porte of the project which his master was contemplating, and which he considered contrary to the interests of which he happened to be at once the too faithful and the too mercenary representative. The ministers of the Porte, guided by narrow views, thought they saw England by this railway already the possessor of Egypt; they needed some means of thwarting the project of the Pasha; they believed they had found what they wanted in certain terms of the firman of investiture granted to the family of Mohammed Ali, and the introduction of the Tanzimat was then formally and officially demanded. Against every right, against all justice, we have seen that during nine months the Porte, supported by the other powers, has succeeded in retarding the establishment of the railway; and although it has at last, by a sort of compromise, authorized the construction, there is a great probability that the Porte will succeed in preventing its completion, or in rendering it of no service to English commerce, by preventing its extension to Suez, if our Government does not again interpose more strongly than it has hitherto done, and cause the rights granted to the family of Mohammed Ali to be duly respected.

To this intervention many may object, on the ground that it is not allowed to a foreign government to interfere in the internal affairs of another country; that for the railway one might employ a friendly interposition, because this railway affects interests common to all nations, and is a European work; but that the Tanzimat is an act of internal administration, a question between the Sultan and his vassal, and that England has consequently no right to interfere officially in such a question.

Our only reply to this objection will be, that the question of the Tanzimat, as we have already hinted, and as we shall soon try to prove, is connected in every point, and for every object, with the question of the railway; that our Government has, therefore, the right of interposing; and, moreover, that it is both its interest and its duty to do so. Who stopped Mohammed Ali in his ambitious designs? Who preserved Egypt to the Porte at the time of the events of 1840? These events have occurred so lately that we cannot have lost sight of them. Did not the Porte, before investing the old Viceroy with the hereditary government of Egypt, communicate the firman of investiture to the representatives of the four allied powers, who examined, approved, and acknowledged it, on behalf of their respective governments, and

1ose approbation and acknowledgment alone
an was sent by the Porte and accepted by the
? have not the four allied powers hereby gua-
at least morally, this firman?   These powers,
our Government at their head, by taking part
ransaction between a Sovereign and his vassal,
so taken upon themselves the engagement to
.e new state of things, which they established,
ually respected on both sides.   The Porte at
nent wishes to violate its engagements; the
of Egypt from among the four powers that
edged his firman and thereby morally guaran-
execution, applies for aid to the one, which
lid the most against his grandfather, but whose
ı are closely connected with the security and
lity of the country which he governs.   If the
ıd not in 1839–40 called the European powers
ı, it would have the right at this moment to
.heir intervention; but having solicited this
questions which may arise between Constan-
and Cairo are no longer mere internal ques-
ınfined to these places, but matters connected
ıropean policy,—in short, European questions.
.vernment has then, we maintain, a right to
e; and its duty and its interests are on the
enforcing this right, for the most important
s, both political and commercial, are at this
at stake.   If the claims of the Porte, which

aim at nothing less than the assimilation of Egypt to the other provinces of the Empire, had for their object to produce the improvement of the country, if the prosperity, tranquillity, and perfect security which both the inhabitants and foreigners now enjoy, were likely to be strengthened, if commerce in general were likely to gain a larger development, there would perhaps then be something specious in our abstaining from all interference; although in good policy, according to our opinion, a regard to rights ought to have precedence of every other consideration. But the case is quite different: justice and right are found on the side of the Viceroy; the interest, properly so called, both of Egypt and of commerce in general, happens to be in accord with the interests of our nation. In order to explain our meaning, it will be necessary to enter into some details respecting the Tanzimat, the consequences which its introduction would produce in Egypt, and the position of the Viceroy in relation to the Sublime Porte.

On the death of the Sultan Mahmoud, his son, the Sultan Abd-ul Medjid, yielding to the generous instincts of his heart, granted a charter to his subjects; this charter, known in all the East under the name of Hatti Sheriff of Gulhané, was solemnly promulgated, and the young Emperor swore to observe it faithfully. By this Hatti Sheriff, or imperial edict, the Sultan, in language as noble as the sentiments which he expressed, guaranteed the life, property, and honour of his subjects; promised to appoint a regular mode for assessing and raising the taxes, and an equally regular method for the levying of soldiers, and the duration of their service. Such were the principles established by the Hatti Sheriff: and we beg the reader not to lose sight of them, for they will be necessary to give an idea of the true state of the question, now pending between the Porte and Egypt.

For the application of these principles, and their reduction to practice, the Supreme Council of Justice, to which the ministers were attached, deliberated and determined on the course to be pursued in civil and commercial proceedings, and in matters of administration and finance; the result of their deliberations was a code at once civil, penal, administrative, and financial, which received the name of Tanzimat, or New Institutions. After the enactments of this Tanzimat, the civil, military, and financial authority in the provinces of the Empire, which was formerly placed in the hands of a single Pasha, was divided between a Pasha as Civil Governor, a Pasha as Military Governor, and a Defterdar, or collector of the taxes.

We have called the Pasha of the province a civil governor; we should rather have called him a chief of the police, for he has no power in the administration. With him is a Council, composed of members partly sent

from Constantinople and partly chosen from among the
inhabitants of the place, which, under his presidency,
judges in every civil and criminal matter, and discusses
and deliberates upon the affairs of the province; but
this Council is not authorized to execute the measures
on which it may decide.   Should the state of the province require certain expenses, and should these expenses exceed the small sum of forty pounds sterling,
the decision of the Council, with the approbation and
through the medium of the Pasha, is transmitted to
the Supreme Council of Constantinople, and accepted
or rejected by it according as the reasons may have
appeared good or bad to functionaries who have never,
perhaps, been out of Constantinople, who even consider employments which would remove them from the
capital in the light of exile, and who probably know
little more than the names of these provinces.

A penal code was promulgated for the whole empire, which is the same for the inhabitants of Arabia,
and for the half-savage tribes of Kurdistan, and for the
peaceable races of Roumelia.

The institutions which establish such a uniform
mode of administration, one vast system of centraliza-
tion, may be good in themselves, and have their intrinsic
worth; we should pronounce them such ourselves, if
we were to judge of the dispositions and character of
the inhabitants of the East by those of the people with
whom we are more immediately connected; we should

also still consider them so, if the Turkish empire were
inhabited only by one and the same race; though even
in such a case we might be induced to ask whether the
Turkish legislators have followed the rules of prudence
in changing all at once, and without any gradation,
institutions which had, so to speak, taken root in the
heart of the people as well as in the soil of the country.

Our opinion is strengthened, when we consider the
heterogeneous elements which compose the vast Turkish
empire. Arabians, Syrians, Kurds, Turks, Albanians,
Greeks, Armenians; all these races, so distinct, so different both in language and character, considering
and treating one another as enemies; is it to be sup-
posed that they can all at once, and without any
transition, receive the same institutions and laws,—be
treated, in short, in the same manner? We should be
inclined, on the ground of these considerations, to say,
that the new Turkish legislators, in forming their
system on the model of the French system, mistook
times and places, and acted rather like empirics, who
prescribe for every sickness the same panacea.

We ought, however, candidly to acknowledge that
it is not our business to determine on the value of
these institutions; we leave the decision of this point
to those whom long study and natural talents have
initiated in the difficult science of the government of
nations. If we have ventured to speak on this point
it has been in relation only to the Egyptian question,

to show that if the Tanzimat is introduced into Egypt,
the Viceroy must lose, as a necessary consequence, the
power and the rank of governor, which the firman has
confirmed to him, and become a mere chief of the
police ; in short, nothing.

The result of these institutions may easily be per-
ceived, not only by those who, like ourselves, have
lived for many years in the East, but by all who have
spent ever so short a time there. Not a single improvement is effected; all is a state of suffering ; nothing
is done. This is the case not merely in the interior
of Asia Minor and of European Turkey, but even in
the great towns on the coast and in the provinces near
to Constantinople, where the difference of race and
character is not so strongly felt, and where the action
of the central Government is more effective. How,
indeed, can the Provincial Councils occupy themselves
in studying the state of the province when, having to
discharge the duties of a civil and criminal tribunal,
they are obliged to employ their time in judging causes
and law-suits ? But even if these Provincial Councils
had both the time, the inclination, and the power to
study the local interests, how could the Supreme
Council of Constantinople, sitting only some hours
each day, have time to study, in all their details, all
the matters of business daily coming before them from
the shores of the Danube to the confines of Arabia?
Can even the Provincial Councils themselves, though

possessing by right the power to deliberate freely on these matters, in reality perform this duty? Those who have seen them in the towns on the coast cannot think so.

The taxes are not assessed on the land, they are levied on the produce, of which the cultivators pay a tithe to the Government. This system, pernicious and demoralizing in itself, inasmuch as it leaves on one side, to the cultivator, a free opportunity to defraud the Government, and on the other, to the officers of the revenue the means of committing many injustices and exactions, or allowing themselves to be bribed, is still further aggravated, without any advantage to the Treasury, by the manner in which the collection of the tithes is farmed out at Constantinople.

We may thus sum up, in two words, the result :—in reference to the administration of the provinces, the entire absence of improvement and progress ; as to the finances, a Treasury paper which the public offices themselves discount at from 3 to 6 per cent., and the decorations of the functionaries taken back by the Government to make money of them.

The state of Egypt presents a striking contrast to that of Turkey. Every one knows the good order and security which there prevail ; it would be idle to speak on this point, except with the object, which may be permitted to us, of impressing on those who may be dazzled by the pretended liberal institutions of Turkey, the observation, that the first want of a people which has for a long time groaned under an arbitrary yoke, harassed and oppressed by a multiplicity of masters, is not liberal institutions; it is tranquillity, a freedom from oppression, security; this also is the first stone on which the future edifice of its civilization can and must rest. In this way Mohamed Ali began. Whilst in Turkey there were no laws for the people, but the will of the Sultan, of his Pashas, of their subordinates, and of the subordinates of their subordinates, in Egypt the Viceroy had compiled a code, had adapted it to the manners of the people whom he governed, had established tribunals, and no person could be executed in Egypt without a previous trial and sentence, passed according to certain prescribed rules, and confirmed by the Viceroy himself. The principle of the Hatti Sheriff of Gulhané, which forbids any functionary to put a person to death arbitrarily, existed in Egypt even before the young Sultan, who established it in Turkey, was born : in that, as in everything, Egypt preceded Constantinople. This extraordinary man, who found his people barbarians and in the state of an infant, treated them as we treat an infant; he gave them tranquillity, opened schools for their instruction, and made the most liberal arrangements to improve their hygeinic state.* He thus provided for

* To show the ignorance of the people, and their indifference on the subject of education, we may mention that the Pasha was obliged

their first wants, and, in order that his reforms might be lasting, he took from our civilization, not its forms and its words, but what the manners of the people could bear, leaving the rest to time and to his descendants. His grandson Abbas, educated in public affairs under the eyes of his grandfather, took up the work where he had left it. The penal code, which Mohamed Ali had compiled and promulgated, and which towards the last year of his administration he had modified, because its first rigour was no longer necessary, was anew modified, and improved by his grandson. At the same time dispossessing the tenants to whom his predecessor had farmed a great part of the lands, he restored these lands to free cultivation, and to their ancient and true proprietors. But it was a small matter to render them free, and the masters of their

to induce parents to send their children to the schools which he had instituted, by offering them money, and by giving also a monthly allowance to the children themselves; and up to this moment every boy educated in the schools of the Government receives, in addition to his gratuitous instruction, a pension, every month, according to his advancement. Moreover, upwards of £25,000 are yearly spent for the purpose of educating young persons in Europe.

Physicians are appointed in every part of Egypt and paid by the Government, for the purpose of improving the hygeinic condition of the country, giving gratuitous attendance to the inhabitants; and the small pox, which formerly committed such ravages in Egypt, has now almost entirely disappeared, vaccination, which is not known in the interior of Turkey, being gratuitously performed in every village by men who receive a remuneration from the government, according to the number of children brought to them.

own lands; it was necessary also to give them the means of turning them to account, and of cultivating them. He has accordingly advanced them considerable sums. Where he has been able to dispense with the immediate levying of the taxes, he has allowed the sums due to accumulate, demanding their payment in small portions from time to time, as the Government may require. He has, moreover, relieved them of the heaviest burden which Mohamed Ali had imposed on them, we mean the Capitation tax, which he has for the greater part abolished.

If we are asked how he has been able to remove so many burdens without diminishing his own resources, we answer, that he has accomplished it by the new development which agriculture has received, and which has produced a remarkable increase in the revenue of the custom-house of Alexandria; by the order and economy introduced into the expenses of the administration; and by the reduction both of the army and navy. These are the measures which enabled him to relieve his people.

Certain articles of commerce were still monopolies in the hands of the Government, on his coming to power these monopolies were removed; the Government, by the mode of collecting the taxes,* being the

* In order to render the payment of taxes by the peasantry more easy to them, they are permitted to pay in kind, which the greater part of them do, as both more convenient and more beneficial to themselves.

B

greatest holder of the products of Egypt, commerce was carried on by a system of favouritism which benefited only certain great merchants, to the detriment of the community and the Government; Artin Bey, the minister of commerce, being interested in the maintenance of this state of things, prevented for some time the introduction of a more liberal system; but his efforts could not succeed long; favouritism was abolished, and by the establishment of public auctions a free competition was opened.

The custom-houses of the interior which impeded commerce were removed; nevertheless, what no free-trader we think can disapprove or complain of, the high duty which Mohamed Ali had towards the latter period of his administration imposed upon slaves, on their admission into Egypt, as a measure tending to put an end to, or at least to diminish, the traffic in Negroes, was maintained. In short, a number of small abuses, too many to be enumerated, imperceptible singly, but which in the mass made themselves strongly felt, were corrected or removed. Egypt had no roads; it is indeed furrowed by a number of navigable canals, so that it does not much feel the want of them; however, in order to facilitate the circulation of the products of the Delta, the Viceroy caused a large causeway to be constructed from the capital of this province to Cairo. This road, and that which he made in the Desert, are the only two which exist in all the East; that which the Turkish Government wished to open between Trebisond and Erzeroum having been abandoned for want of means to complete it. Finally, the railway which, in spite of all the difficulties that he has had to encounter, he wished, and still wishes, to establish, shows how well Abbas understands the interests of his people, and what methods he takes in order to civilize them.

To sum up:—from the time when they groaned beneath the tyranny of the Mamelukes, the Egyptians have gradually passed through a series of improvements, progressing in their material well-being, and advancing towards civilization. The resources of the country, well-managed, are sufficient for its government, and perfect peace and tranquillity prevail throughout the land. How many of us have visited Egypt, in every direction, without an escort, and without danger! We do not wish it to be inferred from the statements we have made as to the beneficial measures adopted by the Government of Egypt that no evils remain to be remedied ; but we do mean to imply that the country is in a state of progressive improvement, and that the present administration is both an enlightened and an able one.

Let us speak now of the claims of the Porte. She wishes to deprive the Viceroy of the power which up to the present moment has been one of his prerogatives, that is, to confirm or annul any sentence of capital punishment passed by the tribunals of the country.

She wishes to efface the name of the local Egyptian Government in all public acts, and to substitute for it her own, and thereby cause justice to be administered in her name. She wishes to deprive the Viceroy of his administrative power, and to transfer this power directly to herself; in one word, to assimilate Egypt to the other provinces, and the Viceroy to the other pashas of the Empire. These two last demands are made in the name of the Tanzimat. This is what the Porte means when she speaks of introducing the Tanzimat into Egypt.

Every impartial person may see the injustice of these claims. What would become of the firman of investiture, should these demands be admitted? Have the Viceroys, or have they not, up to the present time, exercised the administrative power in its full extent in Egypt? And if they have thus exercised it, did they not do so by virtue of this firman? Has the Porte for the last twelve years raised the least objection on this point? Does not this long silence confirm both the letter and the spirit of this firman? The fact alone of the grant of the Government of Egypt to the family of Mohamed Ali is a sufficiently strong proof that the Porte and the allied powers intended, by granting this firman, to make the position of Egypt and its pashas an exception to that of the other provinces and the other pashas of the empire. If we had not the express authority of the text of the firman in confirmation of this fact, the grant alone would be, in our opinion, a conclusive proof of it.

The Porte wishes to annul the name of the local Egyptian Government, she accordingly denies the existence of this local government, and yet the firman says—"*As the zeal and sagacity by which thou art characterized, &c. &c. I grant unto thee the government of Egypt, within its ancient boundaries.*" Language cannot more clearly or positively declare that this government exists, and that it was granted to Mohamed Ali. The allied powers have so fully understood that this Government existed, and had to a certain degree an independent action, that their representatives near him add to their title of Consul-General that of political agent. They are, morever, directly accredited to the Viceroy ; and their *exequatur* is not given by the Porte, but by the Government of the Pasha. If the expressions in the text of the firman had any ambiguity in them, these facts alone would of themselves establish the independent action of the Viceroy in the internal administration of the country. But the text of the firman presents no ambiguity. It will be easy to judge of this by a reference to it. After having enumerated the acts and the qualities which entitle Mohamed Ali to "*the grant of the government of Egypt within its ancient boundaries, together with the additional privilege of hereditary succession,*" the firman recites the conditions annexed to this privilege.

Firman, of February 13, 1841.

Henceforth, when the post shall be vacant, the Government of Egypt shall descend in a direct line, from the elder to the elder, in the male race among the sons and grandsons. As regards their nomination, that shall be made by my Sublime Porte.

If it shall please Providence at any time that the male line should become extinct, as in that case it will devolve upon my Sublime Porte to confer the Government of Egypt on another person, the male children, issue of the daughters of the Governors of Egypt, shall possess no right to, no legal capacity for, the succession to the Government.

Although the Pashas of Egypt have obtained the privilege of hereditary succession, they still must be considered, as far as precedency is concerned, to be on a footing of equality with the other Viziers, they shall be treated like the other Viziers of my Sublime Porte, and they shall receive the same titles as are given to the other Viziers when they are written to.

The principles founded on the laws of security of life, of the security of property, and the preservation of honour, principally recorded in the salutary ordinances of my Hatti Sheriff of Gulhané; all the treaties concluded and to be concluded between my Sublime Porte and the friendly Powers, shall be completely executed in the province of Egypt likewise; and all the regulations made and to be made by my Sublime Porte, shall also be put in practice in Egypt, reconciling them in the best way possible with the local circumstances and with the principles of justice and of equity.

In Egypt, all the taxes, all the revenues, shall be levied and collected in my sovereign name; nevertheless, as the Egyptians are likewise the subjects of my Sublime Porte, and in order that they may not one day be oppressed, the tenths, the duties, and the other taxes which are levied there, shall be so in conformity with the equitable system adopted by my Sublime Porte; and care shall be taken to pay, when the period for payment shall arrive, out of the customs-duties the capitation tax, the tenths, the revenues, and other produce of the province of Egypt, the annual tribute of which the amount is inserted and defined in another Imperial firman.

It being customary to send every year from Egypt provisions in kind to the two Holy Cities, the provisions and other articles, whatever they may be, which have up to this time been sent to each place separately shall continue to be sent thither.

As my Sublime Porte has taken the resolution of improving the coin, which is the soul of the operations of society, and of taking measures so that henceforth there can be no variation either in the alloy or in the value, I grant permission for money to be coined in Egypt; but the gold and silver monies which I permit thee to coin, shall bear my name, and shall resemble in all respects, as regards their determination, value, and form, the monies which are coined here.

In time of peace, 18,000 men will suffice for the internal service of the province of Egypt; it shall not be allowed to increase their numbers. But as the land and sea forces of Egypt are raised for the service of my Sublime Porte, it shall be allowable, in time of war, to increase them to the number which shall be deemed suitable by my Sublime Porte.

The principle has been adopted that the soldiers employed in the other parts of my dominions shall serve for five years, at the end of which term they shall be exchanged for recruits. That being the case, it would be requisite that the same system should also be observed in Egypt in that respect. But with regard to the duration of the service, the dispositions of the people shall be attended to, at the same time that what is required by equity is observed with regard to them.

Four hundred men shall be sent every year to Constantinople, to replace others.

There shall be no difference between the distinguishing marks and the flags of the troops which shall be employed there, and the distinguishing marks and the flags of the other troops of my Sublime Porte. The officers of the Egyptian navy shall have the same distinguishing marks of ranks, and the Egyptian vessels shall have the same flags, as the officers and vessels of this place.

The Governor of Egypt shall appoint the officers of the land and sea forces up to the rank of Colonel, that is to say, of Pashas Miri livi (Brigadier-Generals), and of Pashas Ferik (Generals of Division). With regard to the appointments to ranks higher than these, it will be absolutely necessary to apply for permission for them, and to take my orders thereupon.

Henceforth the Pashas of Egypt shall not be at liberty to build vessels of war without having first applied for the permission of my Sublime Porte, and having obtained from it a clear and positive authority.

As each of the conditions settled as above is annexed to the privilege of hereditary succession, if a single one of them is not executed, that privilege of hereditary succession shall forthwith be abolished and annulled.

The mere reading of this firman shows us how minutely the Porte has pointed out and described all the prerogatives that she reserved to herself in the Egyptian government, which she granted hereditarily to Mohamed Ali. Thus, she has taken care to say that, although the hereditary Pasha of Egypt, he shall be on the same footing, *as far as precedency is concerned,* as the other Viziers; that Egypt shall have an army, but that this army, with the navy, shall be considered *as raised for the Sultan's service*; that there shall be no difference *between the marks and the flags of both countries' troops; that the coins which the Viceroy shall coin shall bear the name of the Sultan; that the taxes shall be levied in his name, and that the Pasha shall pay a tribute out of the total amount.* Everything is then provided for, everything is carefully marked. The condition which attaches to the administration is clear, and requires no comments. The Porte says, that the principles of the Hatti Sheriff, respecting the security of life and property, shall be introduced into Egypt; and the laws made, and to be made, *shall also be put in practice in Egypt, reconciling them, in the best way possible, with the local circumstances, and with the principles of justice and equity.* In truth, we try in vain to reconcile the claims of the Porte with the text of this article of the firman, which she takes as the basis of her demands. We ask ourselves, how this article deprives the Pasha of the power of executing the laws, of causing justice to be administered according to these same laws and in the name of the Egyptian Government, how, in a word, it deprives him of the internal administration of the country? To our eyes, this article is a convincing proof of the power which the Pasha possesses in the internal administration; and we are confirmed in this opinion by observing with what care the Porte separates the political from the administrative action, reserving the first entirely to herself:—"*That all the treaties concluded, and to be concluded, between my Sublime Porte and the friendly powers shall be completely executed in the province of Egypt.*" By these words alone she deprives the Pasha of all political independence. If she had wished it, or if the Pasha had consented to be deprived of all administrative independence also, this fact would have been as clearly established. Instead of that, she contents herself with specifying to him the laws, according to which he is to administer the government of the country. But it may be objected, that this article does not say, in precise terms, that the internal administration belongs to the Viceroy. We ask, in reply to this objection, what means, then, the grant of the firman, the grant of the Government of Egypt to Mohamed Ali and to his family? We may further reply, that the article of the firman which relates to the finances, in like manner does not specify in precise terms that the revenues of Egypt are to be administered by the Viceroy, and, nevertheless, it has not occurred to any one to dispute his possession of this power. Did not the noble lord, who a few days ago quitted the Foreign Office, and whom in 1840 no person can accuse of any partiality in favour of Egypt, declare on two different occasions, before a full Parliament, that the position of Egypt was an exceptional one, and that "*undoubtedly it was the opinion of the Government, which it had expressed to both parties, that the Pasha of Egypt was entitled to make that railroad ' out of his own funds,' according to the forms of the firmau which was granted him in* 1841"?

If the Viceroy has the power of executing any work ' out of his own funds,' it is evident that his funds belong to himself, that he has the administration of them, and that the Porte has no right to meddle with them. She has attempted, however, to do so in reference to the question raised by the railway.

Are not the two articles which refer to the finances and to the administration identical in their form and tenor? As to the finances, the Porte lays down the principle, that the taxes are to be levied in the name of the Sultan, and that a tribute is to be paid; the surplus, of course, remains at the disposal of the Pasha.

As to the administration, she enacts that the principles of the Hatti Sheriff of Gulhané, concerning the security of life and property, shall be introduced into

Egypt; that the laws made, and to be made, shall be, as far as possible, adapted to the local circumstances, and to the rules of justice and equity; and after these formalities shall have been attended to, it is also a matter of course that the administration, according to these laws, remains in the hands of the Pasha.

This subject is so simple and so evident in itself, that all these explanations are wholly needless; but we have thought it right to enter into them, because the Porte denies their evidence. The Porte relies on the second part of this article, in order to colour its claims with an appearance of justice. The first part, referring to the principles of the Hatti Sheriff of Gulhané, were in full operation in Egypt, as we have already said, long before they were established in Constantinople; besides, to our own knowledge, the Pasha has shown no disposition to reject them. The whole difference, therefore, arises upon the second part. But we may remark, at the outset, that the Porte, by this very article, admits certain incompatibilities between her institutions, that is to say, the Tanzimat, and the local circumstances of Egypt; she allows also, that the *principles of justice and equity* ought to regulate their introduction into this country. Let us see, whether, in her present demands, she pays any regard to these incompatibilities, and to these principles of justice and equity. At the very commencement, indeed, of this dispute, she appealed to these principles, and declared her wish only to revise and modify the penal Egyptian code, which to her appeared too rigorous, and to introduce into Egypt some portions of the Tanzimat. Admitting for a moment the justice of her demands, which however we do not concede, can we also admit their suitableness and prudence? When we regard the state of the two countries, and consider the character of their population, we cannot for an instant hesitate in our opinion. Though even her laws and institutions might be good and capable of giving tranquillity to the populations adjoining the capital, which they are not, would it therefore follow that they would be equally good and sufficient for the government of a country inhabited by Fellahs, by Arab settlers, by Bedouins,—races hostile to each other, and who only seek an opportunity for attacking and plundering each other? Not long ago these Arabs and Fellahs, who are now so peaceable, were accustomed to pillage the suburbs of Cairo. Let but the salutary fear which Mohamed Ali inspired cease to affect them, and the ancient scenes of plunder would immediately recommence.*

Does not the state of the provinces of the Empire prove the imprudence of the first demand of the Porte?

---

* It may interest us to know how Napoleon thought and wrote in some remarks which he has left on Egypt:—"The Bedouins peaceably cultivating their lands, or pasturing their cattle, tranquil under a strong government, but the scourges of Egypt under a feeble government."

If Egypt has advanced, if its inhabitants are making progress towards a state of greater civilization, if our mails and our travellers cross the desert in complete security, we are indebted for this improved condition of things to those institutions and laws which the Porte wishes to change; institutions and laws adapted to the character of the country and of its inhabitants. If the desire of the Porte is really a desire for advanced civilization, why not leave an enlightened government to follow the course which under it has so well succeeded? Why wish to make an experiment in Egypt, which has not been successful in any of the Turkish provinces? These are the questions we ask. Why is Egypt so prosperous and flourishing, whilst the other Turkish provinces are in so wretched a state? Are Lebanon and the plains of Syria deficient in fertility? Could not Bagdad, the ancient Mesopotamia, which has the same character of country, the same soil as Egypt, be made, with some labour bestowed upon its cultivation, to rival Egypt in the richness of its products, instead of being a burden on the treasury? We ask every impartial reader, should we not be tempted to say to the Porte, "Try, before pretending to carry out your institutions in Egypt, to cause them to be executed in your own provinces, and to introduce there more order than at present exists?"

Every Englishman is persuaded that the transit

through Egypt is indispensable to us as a nation, and
that the tranquillity and security of that country are
almost as essential to us as the tranquillity and security
of our own ; it is evident that the claims of the Porte
place this security in danger, and it is therefore the
duty of the English Government and people to oppose
these claims. In defending the right of the Viceroy
we defend our own right and our own interest, and
with these also the side of justice. In fact, had the
Porte only proposed, as at first pretended, a slight
revision of the code of Egypt, and the reconciliation of
some of her institutions to the local circumstances of
the country, still leaving the administration of these
laws and of these institutions to the power of the
Pasha, the danger, although great, would not be immi-
nent ; we might then have abstained from interposing
officially, and offered only our friendly services. But
now the question is a different one ; the Porte demands
the annulment of the authority of the Pasha, and herein
is the danger. She demands this annulment in the
name of the Tanzimat and of the article which we have
above recited. She says, "I have the right of introducing my institutions, viz., the Tanzimat, into Egypt,
in reconciling them to the local circumstances. By
the Tanzimat the execution of the laws in the provinces
is under the surveillance of the Provincial Councils,
therefore the Provincial Council of Egypt, as in the
other provinces, must watch over the execution of the

laws, and correspond directly with the Supreme Council
at Constantinople. Moreover, this Supreme Council
of Constantinople is the guardian of the institutions of
the Empire, and every functionary of the Porte accused
of negligence in the exercise of his duties will be tried
and deposed, if the majority of this Supreme Council
pronounce sentence against him; consequently you,
the hereditary Governor of Egypt, will be deposed if
you are found guilty of negligence." Thus the Porte
reasons. But before we reply to this reasoning we
will ask, how many of the Turkish functionaries would
remain in their place if this article of the Tanzimat
were put into execution? In the case, however, of
the Viceroy of Egypt, there is no doubt that it would
be executed. The Turkish ministers have not forgot-
ten the defeats which Egypt has made them undergo;
their hatred is ever ready to manifest itself against the
members of the family of Mohamed Ali, and they all
impatiently await the moment of glutting their hatred,
and satisfying their avidity at the expense of the peasantry and people of Egypt. Now do not the ministers of the Porte see that the claim of subjecting the
Viceroy to the control of the Supreme Council of Constantinople, and of deposing him at the pleasure of the
majority of its members, is an attack on the firman?
The firman points out the cases in which the Pasha
may be deposed; to add another to them is to change
it. The firman, moreover, grants the government of

Egypt to the Viceroy ; is not the attempt to place the execution of the laws under the surveillance of the Council of Cairo and of the Council at Constantinople, in fact, to transfer the authority of the Viceroy to these two Councils? and is not this to change the firman? But the Porte may say, these articles are in the Tanzimat, and the Tanzimat modified may be introduced into Egypt. How! the ministers of the Porte admit incompatibilities between their institutions and the local circumstances of Egypt, and they do not allow that this firman is one of the local circumstances, and the strongest of all; since by it an exceptional position has been created for Egypt and her Viceroy. To concede the justice of their claims, would be to admit that the Tanzimat might annul the firman— that a consequence might annul its cause. The emptiness of such reasoning is immediately apparent.

As for the authority which has been hitherto exercised by the Viceroy of Egypt of confirming or annulling a sentence of capital punishment, we think that for the sake of the tranquillity and security of the country it must be left in the hands of the Pasha. For these reasons the Pasha claims it. As may be seen in a note* which we put at the

---

* If the crime which bears the penalty of capital punishment has been committed in one of the provinces of Egypt, the criminal is at first tried by the religious tribunal, according to the text of the

bottom of this page, the life of the criminal, according
to the mode of proceeding in Egypt, is surrounded by
every possible guarantee ; and as a proof of it, we may
allege what was so truly stated at the meeting held in
the city, respecting the affairs of Egypt, that since the
administration of Abbas no capital execution has taken
place in all Egypt, and that towards the last years of
Mohamed Ali two instances only occurred. But we
should observe, the power of life and death has not, in
the East, the same extension and the same meaning as
in Europe. According to the text of the Turkish religious law, in cases of murder for example, the heirs
of the dead person may grant the life of the murderer,
contenting themselves with the payment of the fine
fixed as the price of blood, and in this case no consti-
tuted power has the right of inflicting capital punish-

religious law, and conjointly also by the civil tribunal. If these two
tribunals find that there is any occasion to apply the punishment of
death, the sentences which they have passed are sent separately to
the great Council of Justice at Cairo. Attached to this council are
two persons from the body of Ulemas. In this council the two
sentences are revised : if they are found to be conformable to justice,
they are anew sent to the council of ministers, who for such cases
associate with themselves the two chiefs of the body of the Ulemas
of Egypt. And it is only after the council of ministers, in con-
junction with the two Ulemas, have pronounced their decision,
that the sentence is sent to the Viceroy, in order to be either confirmed or commuted. It is sufficient for one of these tribunals, either
civil or religious, to pronounce against the capital punishment, and
the sentence cannot take effect.

C

ment on the murderer; but, in like manner, if the heirs do not consent to accept this fine, and demand the death of the culprit, no power, also, has the right of commuting the penalty. Thus, then, in such cases, the right of life and death belongs neither to the Sultan nor to the Viceroy; it is a right of the heirs. This right of life and death can, then, only be exercised in those crimes or offences which are committed against the Government itself. Hence the rareness of a capital execution in Egypt, for the people have still that salutary fear with which the administration of Mohamed Ali inspired them; they know that the Go. vernment has the means of punishing them, of repressing disturbances, and it is this fear and this knowledge which keep them quiet. Remove this influential motive; say to the Fellahs and the Arabs, that the sentence passed on them must, in order to be executed, be sent to Constantinople to be confirmed by the Sultan; destroy, in short, the *prestige* of the Egyptian Government, and ere a long time has elapsed, you will see these races resume their ancient savage instincts.

This is no exaggerated supposition; already, on the mere report that the Tanzimat was going to be introduced, some districts have shown symptoms of insubordination and even of revolt. The customary good order has been disturbed; what would happen if the Tanzimat were introduced? We may confidently affirm, that the Christians would be the first to suffer from the consequences of the change. All the measures of the Porte, since the agitation of this question, have tended to weaken and depreciate the local government in the estimation of the people.

Can we believe that the Arabs and Fellahs have witnessed unmoved almost all the princes of the family of Mohamed Ali abandon, one after another, both their country and the chief of their family, and change their rank as princes for the honour of mingling in the crowd of functionaries at Constantinople? The secret emissaries of the Porte have given them to understand that the government of Abbas had not the means of repressing them; hence the symptoms of which we have just spoken. If this power of life and death, a symbol of authority and not of sovereignty in the East, were withdrawn from the Pasha, the insinuations of the emissaries of Constantinople would be confirmed in their opinion, and all who know the character of the Bedouins and the Fellahs can easily imagine the consequences. The power of life and death in Europe is one of the attributes of the sovereign; but according to Oriental ideas it is not so.

It would not be just to reason according to our European ideas upon habits and customs which are foreign to us. But even allowing that this power is understood in the same manner in Asia as in Europe,

c 2

cannot the sovereign delegate it, and does he not in effect delegate it, as, for instance, in our colonies? Could not the Sultan do the same thing, *considering the local circumstances of the country*, which he allows to be different from those of Turkey? A delegation is not a renunciation, and this right would be no less one of his attributes. As it is absolutely necessary for the security of our mails that there should be in Egypt a strong power, capable of making itself respected by the population, and thus of guaranteeing the safety we require, we think that it is both the duty of our Government and the interest of the English nation not to regard with indifference any circumstance which may tend to weaken the local government of that country.

This Egyptian question, which has unexpectedly arisen, is more important than it at first sight appears; it may change the entire face of affairs in Europe. We have heard some persons who resided a long time in Egypt relate that it was one of the sayings of Mohamed Ali, "Egypt is a bridge thrown between Asia and Europe; England must have a free passage over it, or she must take possession of Egypt." These words of the Pasha are true: Egypt must be tranquil; otherwise, for our communications with India, England must make herself master of the country! And any one may see the consequences of such a situation. It is, then, a question of our own interest

to maintain tranquillity in Egypt; and this tranquillity
can only be secured by a strong government. Does
the Porte, or does the existing government of Egypt,
offer the best guarantees for the attainment of this
object? We shall leave the answer to the readers of
this small pamphlet.

We now proceed to consider the question under
a point of view altogether national, in relation to the
railway. Would the rapidity of our communications
with India gain by granting the claims of the Porte?
We do not now speak of the question of security,
which is the principal point, as we think we have
already said enough upon it; we confine ourselves now
simply to the matter of the railway, and we answer
boldly, and without hesitation—No! We have under
our eyes a small pamphlet, which one of the directors
of the Peninsular and Oriental Steam Navigation
Company published some years ago; he says that
being desirous of obtaining facilities for the transit
across Egypt, he went to Constantinople, and after
three or four months spent in useless efforts, he determined to apply directly to Mohamed Ali, and at the
end of two days, the Viceroy, through the medium of
Baghas Bey, his minister, granted all the facilities
asked for, and which included among other things a
diminution of the transit duty, to which, according to
the commercial treaties of the Porte, the Viceroy was
entitled. This transit-duty was reduced from three to

D

one-half per cent.; and this reduced rate received not upon the opening and inspection of the merchandise at the Custom-house, but upon a simple declaration of the agent of the Company, and the transit has been from that time placed upon a regular system.

We all know that Mohamed Ali himself proposed to establish a railway across the Desert; the rails were even ordered, and yet the works did not take place; our readers will understand the influence which then prevailed to prevent their being undertaken. His grandson finally decides on establishing it. We have learned from the French journals, that the first idea of the Viceroy was to construct a railway from Alexandria to Suez, but the Porte advanced its demands of the Tanzimat, and denied the Viceroy's right to construct this railway, and the Viceroy then confined himself to the plan of constructing it from Alexandria to Cairo only, and represented the work as one of mere internal interest. During nine months, however, the Porte claimed to have the right of granting or refusing its authorization for this railway, hoping that the Pasha, in order to avoid undergoing this formality, would renounce his design. The Pasha, nevertheless, persevered, and his submission and the efforts of our ambassador, who had to contend against the influence of the other cabinets, and against the reluctant inclinations of the Porte, at length extorted this authorization.

However, we have already seen by the extract which
we have given from the speech of Lord Palmerston
in the House of Commons, that the Pasha had the
power to make this railway, without applying to the
Porte for its permission. This fact alone proves the
opposition of the Porte to the project. Besides, a
railway from Alexandria to Cairo is only half of what
is necessary for the rapidity of our communication
with India, and it is nothing for English commerce, as
the greatest difficulties and expenses are with the
transport across the Desert. The Viceroy will, doubt-
less, wish to continue his work, but the claims of the
Porte being once admitted, will he have the power?
Will the Porte of her own accord consent to the
establishment of this railway? Even supposing her
to have the desire to do so, will the foreign influences,
which are the moving-spring of all the actions of
the Porte, put no obstacles in the way? Though at
the present moment the ability of Sir Stratford Can-
ning has given a preponderance to English influence,
can we be sure of always maintaining it?

But supposing all these questions to be resolved in
favour of the railway, supposing even that the security
of the country would not belikely to suffer from the claims
of the Porte, will the Pasha, when he shall have seen
his rights disregarded, and abandoned by the power to
which he has applied for support, consent to establish
it? The claims of the Porte once granted, how many

questions and suppositions, each more doubtful than the other, must we admit to enable us to arrive at a conclusion favourable to the construction of the railway! We will say one thing more: so long as the question now pending is not settled in favour of the Viceroy, we shall not for our own part consider even the railway from Alexandria to Cairo as a "*fait accompli.*" In truth, the Porte, besides its claims embodied in the Tanzimat, requires that the Pasha should consult her and procure her permission in all *delicate* matters. This clause is quite foreign to the firman of investiture; though, indeed, what claim of the Porte is in agreement with it? The term " delicate " is a very elastic one in matters of administration; it may be extended to everything; and this clause admitted, will suffice of itself to raise hindrances to the construction of the railway. It is evident that the Viceroy, in order to complete this work, will require all his resources: according to the text of the authorization which the Porte has granted, and which all the papers have given at length, the Pasha cannot make over the railway to any foreign company, nor can he contract a loan; he will consequently be under the necessity of withdrawing by degrees the advances of money which he has made to the Fellahs, and to collect the arrears due to the government from the old tenants.

Will not this collection of arrears, presented under

Printed in the USA
CPSIA information can be obtained
at www.ICGtesting.com
LVHW061358110823
754771LV00019B/37